The Color of Marriage

15 Principles to Improve Your Marriage

Joe Robinson

authorHOUSE®

AuthorHouse™
1663 Liberty Drive
Bloomington, IN 47403
www.authorhouse.com
Phone: 1-800-839-8640

© 2015 Joe Robinson. All rights reserved.

No part of this book may be reproduced, stored in a retrieval system, or transmitted by any means without the written permission of the author.

Published by AuthorHouse   01/19/2015

ISBN: 978-1-4969-5649-1 (sc)
ISBN: 978-1-4969-5650-7 (e)

Any people depicted in stock imagery provided by Thinkstock are models, and such images are being used for illustrative purposes only. Certain stock imagery © Thinkstock.

Because of the dynamic nature of the Internet, any web addresses or links contained in this book may have changed since publication and may no longer be valid. The views expressed in this work are solely those of the author and do not necessarily reflect the views of the publisher, and the publisher hereby disclaims any responsibility for them.

"Scripture quotations taken from the New American Standard Bible®, Copyright © 1960, 1962, 1963, 1968, 1971, 1972, 1973, 1975, 1977, 1995 by The Lockman Foundation Used by permission." (www.Lockman.org)

"Scripture quotations marked (ESV) are from The Holy Bible, English Standard Version® (ESV®), copyright © 2001 by Crossway, a publishing ministry of Good News Publishers. Used by permission. All rights reserved."

Contents

Dedication vii
Acknowledgements ix
Introduction xi
My Story xix

The 15 Principles 1
Let Your Marriage Represent The Color of Marriage 2
Following God's Plan for Your Marriage is Foundational 10
Make an Effort to Change Old Destructive Behaviors 17
Your Marriage Will Not Get Better Without Learning 24
God Knows What is Best for Us at All Times 31
Do not Let Your Selfishness Corrode Your Marriage 36
Choose a Suitable Time to Talk about Challenging Topics 43
Communicate with your spouse without the hostile language 50
Don't Let the World Pull You In 57
Pray and Expect God to Help You Resolve Your
Unresolved Conflicts 64
Be Willing to Change 68
Do not let your prior experiences destroy the trust and
intimacy of your marriage 74
Do not let your prior experiences destroy the trust and
intimacy of your marriage: Part II 81
God will test you in the areas of your marriage where He
requires you to change or grow 88
God Can See Things That You Cannot (Walk In The Spirit) 94

Dedication

I would like to dedicate this book to my late mother Odelle Harris who made heaven her home when this book was only a thought in my mind and a mere conversation with others.

I would also like to dedicate this book to my wife Rhonda who encouraged me to start the blog that lead to the writing of this book. You can find that blog @ www.thecolorofmarriage.com

Lastly, I would like to dedicate this book to everyone that took the time to read my ideas when I asked them to and to all the married and engaged couples that my wife and I was given the opportunity to help in one way or another.

Acknowledgements

I thank my God, Lord, and Savior Jesus Christ for giving me the desire to write this Christian marriage-learning guide. I pray that this learning guide will help many married, engaged, and potential couples obtain a healthy long-lasting biblical marriage that pleases God and brings Him glory. I also thank my wife Rhonda and my children Precious, Gabrielle, Joe Jr., John, Christopher, Lil Rhonda, and Jaron (that is all of them) for being patience while I took time away from them to write this book.

Introduction

I would like to first thank God for giving me the vision, the wisdom, and the ability to make this Christian marriage-learning guide available to you. This learning guide was designed to help married, engaged, and potential couples obtain a healthy long-lasting biblical marriage that pleases God and brings Him glory. There are several ways in which you and others can use this learning guide to fulfill its intended purpose, which again is to help married, engaged, and potential couples obtain a healthy long-lasting biblical marriage that pleases God and brings Him glory.

First of all, you and your spouse or potential spouse can use this learning guide in your own personal study time with each other. Doing so will help you and your spouse or potential spouse move towards accomplishing the intended purpose of this learning guide. When you and your spouse or future spouse work towards having a marriage that pleases God, you can be sure that it will be pleasing to you and your spouse or potential spouse as well.

Another way that you and others can use this learning guide is in a church or ministry setting. Your pastor and lay leaders can use this learning guide while counseling or encouraging you and others to a healthy long-lasting biblical marriage through the word of God. Your pastor and lay leaders can also use this learning guide for ministries that involves teaching you and other married, engaged, and potential couples about God's plan for marriage.

The last way that I will mention how you and others can use this learning guide is with a Christian coach or Christian counselor. Christian coaches and counselors can use this learning guide to encourage you, the married, engaged, or potential couple, with meeting your goal of having a healthy long-lasting biblical marriage that pleases God and brings Him glory. Christian coaches and counselors can be especially vital when you and your spouse or potential spouse find accomplishing the purpose of this learning guide challenging.

This in no way is an exhaustive list of the ways that you can use this learning guide. I pray that you will be creative and think of other ways that you and others can use this learning guide to help you and other married, engaged, and potential couples fulfill the goal of this learning guide. Please feel free to share your ideas with me at our website, www.thecolorofmarriage.com.

Now that you are aware of some of the ways that you can use this learning guide let us briefly explore what you can expect to receive from its content. The Color of Marriage will make available to you a relevant and diverse set of principles, scriptures, and prayers that will provide biblical solutions pertaining to the conflicts and challenges of marriage. When you study and use these principles, scriptures, and prayers in conjunction with application, fulfilling the purpose of this learning guide will become a reality in your marriage.

Take the following into consideration -

A substantial amount of conflict within your marriage will not be avoided or resolved until you start thinking, believing, and consciously living out the word of God that identifies the conflicts and challenges you are or will be experiencing within your marriage.

Consider the following scriptures -

Hebrews 4:12 "For the word of God is living, and active, and sharper than any two-edged sword, and piercing even to the dividing of soul and spirit, of both joints and marrow, and is able to discern the thoughts and intentions of the heart." (WEB)

Jeremiah 23:29 "Is not my word like fire, declares the LORD, and like a hammer that breaks the rock in pieces?" (ESV)

James 1:25 "But one who looks intently at the perfect law, the law of liberty, and abides by it, not having become a forgetful hearer but an effectual doer, this man will be blessed in what he does." (NASB)

2 Timothy 3:16-17 "[16] All Scripture is breathed out by God and profitable for teaching, for reproof, for correction, and for training in righteousness, [17] that the man of God may be complete, equipped for every good work. (ESV)

Reflection Question

Thinking about the conflicts and challenges that you are having in your marriage or potential marriage right now, what scriptures do you believe will help you resolve those conflicts and challenges? Try to find at least two to three passages of scripture that relate to your most recent pressing conflicts or challenges.

_____

_____

_____

_____

_____

_____

_____

_____

_____

_____

_____

_____

_____

_____

_____

_____

_____

_____

Reflection Challenge

Now that you have selected a few passages of scripture that you believe will help you with resolving the present conflicts and challenges of your marriage or potential marriage, commit them to memory. Post these scriptures in a place where you will see them on a regular basis and be ready to put them into action the next time these conflicts and challenges come up.

_____
_____
_____
_____
_____
_____
_____
_____
_____
_____
_____
_____
_____
_____
_____
_____

The Reason

The Color of Marriage was written so that you and I would learn the habit of making a conscious effort to live out the Word of God in our marriages. When you trust in the word of God and consciously live it out, you will find real life solutions to the various conflicts and challenges of your marriage. These are the kinds of conflicts and challenges that will prevent your marriage from reaching its greatest potential if they go unresolved. If these conflicts and challenges go unresolved long-term, they will ultimately diminish, damage, and even destroy your marriage and many times your character as well. I believe there would be fewer divorces in the Christian Community if we had the biblical principles of The Color of Marriage hidden in our hearts and ready for use during times of conflict and challenge in our marriages.

Consider the following scriptures –

Psalm 119:11 "I have stored up your word in my heart, that I might not sin against you." (ESV)

Psalm 40:8 "I delight to do Your will, O my God; Your Law is within my heart.'" (NASB)

REFLECTIONS

Write a prayer to God that directly reflects the concerns that you have regarding your marriage. Be open and honest and do not neglect to mention the specific situations that are hindering the growth and quality of your marriage.

REFLECTIONS

My Story

I remember the first time I made a conscious effort to use scripture to resolve a conflict my wife Rhonda and I was having. We were driving home from school and I was elevating my voice to desperately get my point across to her concerning something she had said earlier that offended me. She was not responding to me very well and for that reason my anger was starting to escalate. Sometime after that, The Holy Spirit put 1 Peter 3:7 in my mind which declares:

> "Likewise, husbands, live with your wives in an understanding way, showing honor to the woman as the weaker vessel, since they are heirs with you of the grace of life, **so that your prayers may not be hindered."** *(ESV)*

The last part of that verse is what captured my attention. From that moment on, I was on a quest to apply this passage of scripture so that I would stop over powering my wife by elevating my voice to get her to see my point of view. I wrote the scripture down and even mentioned to her the next day that I was trying to put this verse into action. I did not want to continue raising my voice at her again and cause her to feel insecure and over powered. It took some time and some mistakes before I would become somewhat proficient at not raising my voice when I got upset with her.

At the same time, the Holy Spirit had me working on applying **James 1:19-20 and Ephesians 4:26**, concerning anger. I understand now that I had to also apply these scriptures as well before I could become soundly proficient at living out **1 Peter 3:7**.

REFLECTIONS

Before we move on to the next portion of my story, I would like for you to think for a moment and write about some of the actions and behaviors that you may need to change so that your marriage can get better.

Back to my story

At this point:

1. I was no longer just praying and haphazardly trying to apply scriptures when I thought of them and hoping that I would change.
2. I was now putting forth a conscious effort to submit to the Holy Spirit and listen to what He was telling me.
3. I was now learning how to change my old methods of resolving conflict.
4. I was now learning to accept and live out (apply) God's way of resolving conflict through His word.
5. I was now in the process of moving my marriage to greatness, since I was no longer restricting my marriage from reaching its greatest potential through unhealthy behaviors.

This is what The Color of marriage is all about, helping you and I make a conscious effort to live out the commands of scripture so that we can move our marriages to their greatest potential. Coming to the place where you have faith in The Word of God and make a conscious effort to live out the instructions of the word of God, even when it becomes difficult, is a great place to be especially when you want to honor God and bless yourself with a marriage that you can **move to greatness**. I would love to see you **"Move Your Marriage to Greatness"** through the process of reading, learning, and applying these biblical principles, which is equal to **"Marriage Replenishment"**.

Consider the following scripture -

Romans 12:1-2 "¹Therefore I urge you, brethren, by the mercies of God, to present your bodies a living and holy sacrifice, acceptable to God, which is your spiritual service of worship. ²And do not be conformed to this world, but be transformed by the renewing of your mind, so that you may prove what the will of God is, that which is good and acceptable and perfect." (NASB)

REFLECTIONS

Write your story. Remind yourself of why you married your spouse or want to marry your potential spouse. As you write, write about some of the best moments that you were able to share with your spouse or potential spouse. Talk about your wedding day, a special trip, or maybe how your spouse helped you through a hard time in your life.

REFLECTIONS

Making Good Use of The Color of Marriage

The content of The Color of Marriage was written to allow room for the Holy Spirit to speak directly to the heart of the reader. In the end when you have read each portion of the marriage principle, you would be wise to study, meditate, and ask God for His wisdom. You can pray a prayer like David did in Psalm 25:4 "Make me to know your ways, O LORD; teach me your paths." (ESV). I believe that God will honor this prayer and provide to you the necessary information you will need to carry out the application of each principle.

Consider the following scriptures –

John 14:26 – "But the Counselor, the Holy Spirit, whom the Father will send in my name, he will teach you all things, and will remind you of all that I said to you." (WEB)

1 Corinthians 3:16 – "Do you not know that you are a temple of God and that the Spirit of God dwells in you?"

Galatians 5:16-17 – ¹⁶"But I say, walk by the Spirit, and you will not carry out the desire of the flesh ¹⁷For the flesh sets its desire against the Spirit, and the Spirit against the flesh; for these are in opposition to one another, so that you may not do the things that you please".

Take the following into consideration -

You cannot and more than likely will not be successful in fulfilling the goal of this learning guide unless you are willing to submit to the counsel of the following critical passage of scripture from Psalm 1. Therefore, I pray that you will be wise and make every possible effort to meet the goals that God has set for you and your marriage.

Psalm 1:1-2 says – "¹ How blessed is the man who does not walk in the counsel of the wicked, Nor stand in the path of sinners, Nor sit in the seat of scoffers! ² But his delight is in the law of the LORD, And in His law he meditates day and night. (NASB)

REFLECTIONS

Considering the passages of scripture that you have just read, write about how the Holy Spirit and The Word of God can help you overcome the obstacles that will challenge your efforts of meeting the goal of this learning guide. Don't forget to mention yourself in the equation of obstacles, because we all have a tendency to get in our own way.

_____

_____

_____

_____

_____

_____

_____

_____

_____

_____

_____

_____

_____

_____

_____

_____

REFLECTIONS

The 15 Principles

(1) Let Your Marriage Represent The Color of Marriage
(2) Following God's Plan for Your Marriage is Foundational
(3) Make an Effort to Change Old Destructive Behaviors
(4) Your Marriage Will Not Get Better Without Learning
(5) God Knows What's Best for Us at All Times
(6) Do not Let Your Selfishness Corrode Your Marriage
(7) Choose a Suitable Time to Talk about Challenging Topics
(8) Communicate with your spouse without the hostile language
(9) Don't Let the World Pull You In
(10) Pray and Expect God to Help You Resolve Your Unresolved Conflicts
(11) Be Willing to Change
(12) Do not let your prior experiences destroy the trust and intimacy of your marriage
(13) Do not let your prior experiences destroy the trust and intimacy of your marriage: Part II
(14) God will test you in the areas of your marriage where He requires you to change or grow.
(15) God Can See Things That You Cannot (Walk In The Spirit)

(1) Principle: Let Your Marriage Represent The Color of Marriage

The Color of Marriage is the act of living out your marriage in a way that pleases God and brings Him glory. God created the institution of marriage and for this reason; your marriage or potential marriage must be about pleasing Him and bringing Him glory. Every time you willingly choose to practice the principles and concepts that God developed for your marriage, He will see The Color of Your Marriage.

1. Does your marriage represent The Color of Marriage? In other words, is it pleasing to God and does it bring Him glory.

_____

_____

_____

_____

_____

_____

The Color of Marriage

2. Why, in your opinion, is it important for you to live out your marriage in away that pleases God and brings Him glory?

_____

_____

_____

_____

_____

_____

Consider the following scriptures –

Colossians 1:16 "For by Him all things were created, both in the heavens and on earth, visible and invisible, whether thrones or dominions or rulers or authorities-- all things have been created through Him and for Him." (NASB)

Matthew 19:4-6 "⁴And He answered and said, "Have you not read that He who created them from the beginning MADE THEM MALE AND FEMALE, ⁵and said, 'FOR THIS REASON A MAN SHALL LEAVE HIS FATHER AND MOTHER AND BE JOINED TO HIS WIFE, AND THE TWO SHALL BECOME ONE FLESH'? ⁶"So they are no longer two, but one flesh. What therefore God has joined together let no man separate."" (NASB)

Matthew 5:16 "Let your light shine before men in such a way that they may see your good works, and glorify your Father who is in heaven." (NASB)

1 Peter 2:12 "Keep your behavior excellent among the Gentiles, so that in the thing in which they slander you as evildoers, they may because of your good deeds, as they observe them, glorify God in the day of visitation." (NASB)

Joe Robinson

Hebrews 13:4 "Marriage is to be held in honor among all, and the marriage bed is to be undefiled; for fornicators and adulterers God will judge." (NASB)

Psalm 127:1 "Unless the LORD builds the house, They labor in vain who build it; Unless the LORD guards the city, The watchman keeps awake in vain." (NASB)

REFLECTIONS

Thinking about the question, "Does your marriage represent The Color of Marriage"? Can you think of at least three details about your marriage or potential marriage that pleases God and at least three details about your marriage or potential marriage that may not bring Him Glory?

Joe Robinson

REFLECTIONS

(1) Prayer for Let Your Marriage represent The Color of Marriage

Meditate on the following scripture -

Colossians 1:10 "so that you will walk in a manner worthy of the Lord, to please Him in all respects, bearing fruit in every good work and increasing in the knowledge of God;" (NASB)

Father God we pray that our marriage will be pleasing to you and that it will bring you glory. Teach us and give us the desire Father to live out our marriage in this way. Father you know there will be times when we will not want to do this for whatever reason, so when this becomes a reality please give us the ability and the desire to do your will and not our own. May our marriage be a reflection of what you want it to be from now on. Thank you for hearing and answering our prayer and it is in the name of Jesus that we pray. Amen

Take the following into consideration –

Let everything that you do in your marriage bring glory to God as much you can.

Joe Robinson

REFLECTIONS

Write about how this prayer and passage of scripture can help you and your spouse live out your marriage in a way that pleases God and brings Him glory.

REFLECTIONS

(2) Principle: Following God's Plan for Your Marriage is Foundational

When you begin to learn and follow God's plan for your marriage and practice not griping about doing so, your marriage will start to blossom and grow. God wants you and your spouse to become one cohesive unit that symbolizes the relationship that Jesus Christ has with His Church. Husbands are to love their wives and wives are to respect their husbands and allow them to take the lead in the marital relationship.

Consider the following scriptures -

Philippians 2:14 "Do all things without grumbling or disputing;" (NASB)

Proverbs 3:5-6 "⁵Trust in the LORD with all your heart And do not lean on your own understanding. ⁶In all your ways acknowledge Him, And He will make your paths straight." (NASB)

Psalm 1:1-3 "¹Blessed is the man who walks not in the counsel of the wicked, nor stands in the way of sinners, nor sits in the seat of scoffers; ²but his delight is in the law of the LORD, and on his law he meditates day and night. ³He is like a tree planted by streams of water that yields its fruit in its season, and its leaf does not wither. In all that he does, he prospers." (ESV)

The Color of Marriage

Ephesians 5:22-24 "²²Wives, submit to your own husbands, as to the Lord. ²³ For the husband is the head of the wife even as Christ is the head of the church, his body, and is himself its Savior ²⁴ Now as the church submits to Christ, so also wives should submit in everything to their husbands" (ESV)

Ephesians 5:25-32 "²⁵ Husbands, love your wives, as Christ loved the church and gave himself up for her, ²⁶that he might sanctify her, having cleansed her by the washing of water with the word, ²⁷so that he might present the church to himself in splendor, without spot or wrinkle or any such thing, that she might be holy and without blemish. ²⁸In the same way husbands should love their wives as their own bodies. He who loves his wife loves himself. ²⁹For no one ever hated his own flesh, but nourishes and cherishes it, just as Christ does the church, ³⁰because we are members of his body. ³¹Therefore a man shall leave his father and mother and hold fast to his wife, and the two shall become one flesh. ³²This mystery is profound, and I am saying that it refers to Christ and the church." (ESV)

Joe Robinson

REFLECTIONS

Considering the passages of scripture that you have just read, write about why you are willing or not willing to follow God's plan for your marriage. Be specific with your reasons of why you are or are not willing to follow God's plan.

The Color of Marriage

REFLECTIONS

(2) Prayer for Following God's Plan for Marriage is Foundational

Meditate on the following scripture -

Proverbs 19:21 "Many plans are in a man's heart, But the counsel of the LORD will stand." (NASB)

Father may the plan and purpose of our marriage be your plan and purpose. We ask that you change the direction of our hearts so that we will desire to have our marriage reflect the relationship that Jesus has with the Church, His body. Father you know about all of the obstacles that we will face that will try to prevent us from following your plan and because of this we ask that you give to us everything that we need to continue on without giving up or giving in. We need your love, your mercy, and your grace, because without these Father we will surely fail to have a marriage that reflects your plan and purpose. It is in Jesus name that we pray. Amen

Take the following into consideration –

Marriage is a God ordained relationship where two people come together and strive to work out their differences to become one with each other.

REFLECTIONS

Write about how this prayer and passage of scripture can help you and your spouse to start or continue to follow God's plan for marriage.

Joe Robinson

REFLECTIONS

(3) Principle: Make an Effort to Change Old Destructive Behaviors

It is possible to break the cycle of the long-term negative behaviors that are disrupting or destroying your marriage. Your responsibility is to recognize your negative behaviors through the following sources:

1. **Acknowledgment** – Write down and acknowledge your negative behaviors that are disrupting and/or destroying your marriage.
2. **Prayer and meditation** - If you are somehow unaware of the disruptive or destructive behaviors that you may have, pray and listen, so that God can help you recognize those behaviors.

Once you have created your list, ask and allow God to make the necessary changes within you while you make an effort to behave differently towards your spouse and in your marriage every day.

Consider the following scriptures -

Proverbs 28:13 "Whoever conceals his transgressions will not prosper, but he who confesses and forsakes them will obtain mercy." (ESV)

Mark 10:27 "Jesus looked at them and said, "With man it is impossible, but not with God. For all things are possible with God." (ESV)

2 Corinthians 5:17 "Therefore if any man *be* in Christ, *he is* a new creature: old things are passed away; behold, all things are become new." (KJV)

1 Peter 1:14-15 "[14] As obedient children, do not be conformed to the passions of your former ignorance [15] but as he who called you is holy, you also be holy in all your conduct," (ESV)

Read Romans 12:1-2 and explain the course of action that God wants you to take in this passage of scripture concerning changing old destructive behaviors.

REFLECTIONS

Write down your thoughts about what you have just read. Make sure that you leave room to write down the behaviors that may come to your mind as God reveals them to you.

Joe Robinson

REFLECTIONS

(3) Prayer for Make an Effort to Change Old Destructive Behaviors

Meditate on the following scriptures -

Psalm 139:23-24 "²³ Search me, O God, and know my heart! Try me and know my thoughts! ²⁴ And see if there be any grievous way in me, and lead me in the way everlasting!" (ESV)

Lamentations 3:40 "Let us test and examine our ways, and return to the LORD!" (ESV)

Father, cover us with your Love, Grace, and, Mercy and reveal to us the behaviors that we have that are destroying or hurting our marriage. Father, please give us the desire and ability to put an end to our known and unknown destructive behaviors. Help us Father God to understand that without You, Your Son Jesus, and Your Holy Spirit our attitude and behavior towards our marriage will never change. We want to become the people that you desire for us to become within our marriage and we pray that we will make all of the necessary steps to make this happen. Thank you Father and it is in Jesus name that we pray. Amen

Take the following into consideration –

Being willing to change the behaviors that affect your marriage in a negative way is part of living out your marriage in a way that pleases God and brings Him Glory.

Joe Robinson

REFLECTIONS

Write about how this prayer and passages of scripture can help you and your spouse change any behaviors that either of you may or may not be willing to change

REFLECTIONS

(4) Principle: Your Marriage Will Not Get Better Without Learning

Learning how to have a better marriage is essential. We learn how to improve ourselves in many areas of our lives and somehow we forget to learn how to improve our marriages.

The health of any marriage, especially a broken one, depends on what the marriage is being fed. We all know what happens when we feed our natural bodies foods that are unhealthy. Our bodies will begin to decline in health and start failing in many areas over time. The same applies to our marriages. When you fail to consistently feed your marriage the information that it needs to stay healthy, it too will begin to decline in health and start failing in many areas.

Consider the following scriptures –

Proverbs 1:7 – "The fear of the LORD is the beginning of knowledge; fools despise wisdom and instruction."

Proverbs 1:5 – "A wise man will hear and increase in learning, And a man of understanding will acquire wise counsel." (NASB)

Proverbs 8:33 – "Hear instruction and be wise, and do not neglect it." (ESV)

Proverbs 15:14 – "The heart of him who has understanding seeks knowledge, but the mouths of fools feed on folly." (ESV)

Proverbs 15:31 – "He whose ear listens to the life-giving reproof Will dwell among the wise." (ESV)

1 Peter 3:7 – "Likewise, husbands, live with your wives in an understanding way, showing honor to the woman as the weaker vessel, since they are heirs with you of the grace of life, so that your prayers may not be hindered." (ESV)

Proverbs 19:14 – "House and wealth are inherited from fathers, but a prudent wife is from the LORD." (ESV)

Joe Robinson

REFLECTIONS

Write about why it is important to you, to learn how to improve your marriage. Once you are done, write about why your spouse believes it is important to improve your marriage. Share your findings with your spouse and work together to come up with a plan for improving your marriage that works for the two of you.

REFLECTIONS

(4) Prayer for Your Marriage Will Not Get Better Without Learning

Meditate on the following scripture -

Proverbs 4:13 – "Keep hold of instruction; do not let go; guard her, for she is your life." (ESV)

Father let us not be full of pride and refuse to learn how to improve our marriage because of it. May we humble ourselves and turn to you, so that we can lean and depend on your knowledge to keep our marriage sustained and healthy. Forgive us Father for resisting and (or) rebelling against the knowledge that you gave to us through your word and Holy Spirit that would have helped us to improve our marriage. Help us Father to discontinue this practice and learn to ultimately trust you and have faith in what is written in your Holy Word, the Bible. It is in the name of Jesus that we pray. Amen.

Take the following into consideration -

You consistently feed your body what it needs, because you see the value in it. You consistently feed your mind what it needs, because you also see the value in it. We it comes to your marriage you must always see the value in consistently feeding your marriage what it needs as well.

REFLECTIONS

Write about how this prayer and passage of scripture can help you and your spouse learn and understand the need to improve your marriage on a regular basis.

Joe Robinson

REFLECTIONS

(5) Principle: God Knows What is Best for Us at All Times

God Knows Best

I remember as a little boy watching a television program called Father Knows Best, back when it was safe for children to watch television unmonitored. The show, according to my remembrance of it, was about an all-American father whose decisions revolved around what would best benefit his household. He was well respected by his wife and children and he demonstrated the utmost love for them in all that he did. The relationship that he and his family had on screen could have been mirrored by many who watched the show, and probably was.

The purpose I have in taking the time to mention this television program is to illustrate the kind of relationship that God can and wants to have with you and me. Surely, God loves and cares for us far more than the father of this program could have ever demonstrated on a television screen; but nonetheless it is a simple example of the love and care that God wants to share with you and me. God, unlike the father of this show, actually knows what is best for us and wants us to lean and depend on Him so that He can navigate us through life according to what He knows is best for us.

God instructs us in Proverbs 3:5-6 to do three things and once we have accomplished these three directives He promises to do one awesome and incredible thing in return.

1. He says first that we should trust Him with our whole heart.

Our heart is like an invisible reservoir within us where we collect and recall knowledge concerning the manner in which we will live our life. God wants our reservoirs to be filled with the knowledge that will cause us to trust Him.

All disbelief that we have allowed to become registered into the reservoirs of our hearts must be removed by the registering of knowledge that supersedes all registered disbelief in God.

2. We should not depend completely on our own understanding.

We may think that we have a clear understanding of what we are to do in life and this is especially true when we have facts that support our position. God says that we are not to rely completely on these facts and our understanding of them.

3. We are to acknowledge Him in our decision making process.

God wants to lead you in the decision-making process of your life journey. God wants to and is willing to guide you through your life challenges and to share His wisdom with you in every aspect of your life. What you may think is a clear-cut answer to a problem may not always be correct. You should rely on God who, through His infinite wisdom and knowledge, knows what lies ahead that you cannot see because of your lack of knowledge of future events.

4. God will then give you the directions that you very much need.

This is the foundation that you must stand on if you are to have success in your marriage. God has a plan for marriage that you must follow. You must be willing to walk in His plan, even when you think that you have a better plan or that His plan makes no sense to you.

Consider the following scriptures –

John 3:16 – "For God so loved the world, that he gave his one and only Son, that whoever believes in him should not perish, but have eternal life." (WEB)

Romans 5:8 "But God demonstrates His own love toward us, in that while we were yet sinners, Christ died for us." (NASB)

Jeremiah 9:23-24 "²³ Thus says the LORD: "Let not the wise man boast in his wisdom, let not the mighty man boast in his might, let not the rich man boast in his riches, ²⁴ but let him who boasts boast in this, that he understands and knows me, that I am the LORD who practices steadfast love, justice, and righteousness in the earth. For in these things I delight, declares the LORD." (ESV)

Take the following into consideration -

When you and your spouse agree to entrust God with your marriage, it will succeed. Choosing to depend on God to preserve your marriage is a wise decision. Do you believe that God can restore and maintain the security of your marriage? I surely hope that you do. In an article that I wrote, entitled *"Hope"*, I write about how God restored hope to my marriage at a time when my wife and I decided to trust Him with our marriage. You can find that article at the following web address www.thecolorofmarriage.com. **God is not in the business of failing**. You can certainly depend on Him to do what His Word says that He will do.

Joe Robinson

REFLECTIONS

Considering what you have just read, write about why you are going to trust God with your marriage.

REFLECTIONS

(6) Principle: Do not Let Your Selfishness Corrode Your Marriage

If you knew where to get invaluable information that would improve your marriage, would you go and get that information and then refuse to use it because the invaluable information would cause you to stop a behavior that benefited you, but was harmful to your marriage.

You do this when you read or hear instructions from God's word concerning your marriage and refuse to adhere to what you are told. You decline to abide by the instructions you hear and continue to walk in your destructive ways. You rationalize why your behavior is necessary and get the approval of others who are of the same mind so that you can be justified to continue in your behavior instead of submitting to God and choosing to change your behavior.

Consider the following scriptures –

Philippians 2:3-4 – "³Do nothing from selfishness or empty conceit, but with humility of mind regard one another as more important than yourselves; ⁴do not merely look out for your own personal interests, but also for the interests of others." (NASB)

Proverbs 15:32 – "Whoever ignores instruction despises himself, but he who listens to reproof gains intelligence." (ESV)

Colossians 3:5-6 "⁵ Put to death therefore what is earthly in you: sexual immorality, impurity, passion, evil desire, and covetousness, which is idolatry. ⁶ On account of these the wrath of God is coming" (ESV)

REFLECTIONS

Write about how your marriage can benefit from changing selfish behaviors that diminishes the quality of your marriage.

The Color of Marriage

REFLECTIONS

(6) Prayer for Do not let your Selfishness corrode your Marriage

Meditate on the following scripture -

Psalm 51:10 "Create in me a clean heart, O God, and renew a right spirit within me." (ESV)

Father God help me to accept your will for my marriage and not depend on, nor desire to walk in my own selfish will that only brings harm and does nothing good to my marriage. Please forgive me for hurting (your spouse's name) and also please give (your spouse's name) a heart to forgive me when I make my apology to (your spouse's name). Search my heart and clean out all that you find that is not beneficial to my marriage and help me to endure and desire the process. Thank you for your mercy and grace and I pray this in the name of your Son Jesus, amen.

Take the following into consideration –

Marriage is about two selfless people working together to become one, not two selfish people trying to get their own way. (Rhonda Robinson)

REFLECTIONS

Write about how this prayer and passage of scripture can help you and your spouse change selfish behaviors that will corrode your marriage.

Joe Robinson

REFLECTIONS

(7) Principle: Choose a Suitable Time to Talk about Challenging Topics

Do you believe any time is appropriate to have a conversation with your spouse about a subject that could cause conflict? There is always a time and place for everything. You would be wise to choose a suitable time frame to bring up topics that most likely will cause some type of conflict.

Consider the following scriptures -

Proverbs 25:11 "A word fitly spoken is like apples of gold in settings of silver." (WEB)

Proverbs 15:23b "How good is a word at the right time!" (WEB)

Philippians 2:4 "do not merely look out for your own personal interests, but also for the interests of others" (NASB).

Philippians 2:3 "Do nothing from selfishness or empty conceit, but with humility of mind regard one another as more important than yourselves;" (NASB)

Proverbs 14:8a "The wisdom of the prudent is to think about his way," (WEB)

Ecclesiastes 7:8 "Better is the end of a thing than its beginning. The patient in spirit is better than the proud in spirit." (WEB)

Galatians 5:22 "But the fruit of the Spirit is love, joy, peace, patience, kindness, goodness, faithfulness," (NASB)

REFLECTIONS

Considering what you have just read, write about how you can improve your marriage by finding a healthier way to introduce and discuss topics that can potentially cause friction when discussed.

Joe Robinson

REFLECTIONS

(7) Prayer for Choose a Suitable Time to Talk about Challenging Topics

Meditate on the following scripture –

Colossians 3:12 "So, as those who have been chosen of God, holy and beloved, put on a heart of compassion, kindness, humility, gentleness and patience;" (NASB)

Many times Father God I am compelled by my own sinful desires to vent my frustrations at (your spouse's name) without notice and consideration of (your spouse's name) feelings. Help me Father to stop erupting my full range of negative emotions at (your spouse's name) and choose rather to be kind, gentle, compassionate, patience, and humble when I need to talk with (your spouse's name) about a subject or situation that could lead to conflict. I also ask that you forgive me of this sinful behavior and restore the damaged portions of our marriage that I have caused because of this behavior. It is in the name of Jesus that I pray, amen.

Take the following into consideration –

Every marriage will be challenged with difficulties that will either hinder the growth of the marriage or prevent the marriage from reaching its greatest potential unless the difficulties of the marriage can be resolved. Therefore make every effort to spend time investing in your marriage so that you will find resolutions to the difficulties of your marriage and begin moving your marriage to its greatest potential.

Joe Robinson

REFLECTIONS

Write about how this prayer and passage of scripture can help you and your spouse communicate better during discussions that could possibly lead to conflict.

The Color of Marriage

REFLECTIONS

(8) Principle: Communicate with your spouse without the hostile language

Communication between you and your spouse may not be at its best at times, especially when communication killers are being utilized. Talking with a sense of arrogance, speaking in a manner that belittles your spouse, and not being concerned about the words you speak are the types of communication killers that I am referring to. Therefore, whenever you and your spouse are communicating with each other, make sure your speech does not represent a communication killer.

Consider the following scriptures -

James 4:1 "What causes quarrels and what causes fights among you? Is it not this, that your passions are at war within you?" (ESV)

Ephesians 4:29 "Let no corrupting talk come out of your mouths, but only such as is good for building up, as fits the occasion, that it may give grace to those who hear." (ESV)

Proverbs 21:23 "Whoever keeps his mouth and his tongue keeps himself out of trouble." (ESV)

Proverbs 10:19 "When there are many words, transgression is unavoidable, But he who restrains his lips is wise." (NASB)

Romans 14:19 "So then, let us follow after things which make for peace, and things by which we may build one another up." (WEB)

Joe Robinson

REFLECTIONS

Considering the passages of scripture that you have just read, write about how you can remove the hostile language and communication killers from your conversations with your spouse.

REFLECTIONS

(8) Prayer for Communicate with your spouse without the hostile language

Meditate on the following scriptures -

Colossians 3:12-14 ¹²"Put on then, as God's chosen ones, holy and beloved, compassionate hearts, kindness, humility, meekness, and patience, ¹³bearing with one another and, if one has a complaint against another, forgiving each other; as the Lord has forgiven you, so you also must forgive. ¹⁴And above all these put on love, which binds everything together in perfect harmony." (ESV)

Father, I ask that you empower (your spouse's name) and I to make an effort to communicate with each other without becoming hostile towards one another in our attitudes, expressions, and words. While we make the effort to change this unhealthy habit, I ask that you teach us how to resolve our conflicts and challenges without utilizing communication killers. Help us to understand that communication killers do nothing but worsen the issues that are affecting our marriage. May we be gracious in our communication with each other and I pray this prayer in the name of Jesus, Amen.

Take the following into consideration –

Have you ever wondered why your spouse refuses to listen and respond to you during times of conflict or challenge? Maybe it could be that the words that are coming out of your mouth are crushing your spouse's spirit to the point that they have no other reasonable option to chose from.

REFLECTIONS

Write about how this prayer and passage of scriptures can help you and your spouse communicate with each other without hostility and the utilization of communication killers.

Joe Robinson

REFLECTIONS

(9) Principle: Don't Let the World Pull You In

Don't let the culture or society cause you to be embarrassed because the principles of your marriage appear strange to them. The people that you meet, even many of those who call themselves Christians, and your friends will make fun of you because you do not operate your marriage as they do theirs. God, who is your Heavenly Father and Creator of all humans, has set the standard for how He wants you to operate in your marriage in His Word. The people who are living according to this world's standard will not understand God's standard. So resolve to know that God knows best and continue living as God called you to live within your marriage and let God take care of the rest.

Consider the following Scriptures-

John 15:19 – "If you were of the world, the world would love you as its own; but because you are not of the world, but I chose you out of the world, therefore the world hates you." (ESV)

1 Peter 4:3-5 – "[3]For we have spent enough of our past time doing the desire of the Gentiles, and having walked in lewdness, lusts, drunken binges, orgies, carousing, and abominable idolatries. [4]They think it is strange that you don't run with them into the same excess of riot, blaspheming: [5]who will give account to him who is ready to judge the living and the dead." (WEB)

1 John 4:5-6 – "⁵They are of the world: therefore they speak of the world, and the world hears them. ⁶ We are from God, and whoever knows God listens to us; but whoever is not from God does not listen to us. This is how we recognize the Spirit of truth and the spirit of falsehood." (WEB)

1 Corinthians 15:33 – Do not be deceived: "Bad company ruins good morals." (ESV)

The Color of Marriage

REFLECTIONS

Write about why it is important to disregard the conversations of those who will tease and ridicule you for living according to God's standard and not theirs.

Joe Robinson

REFLECTIONS

(9) Prayer for Don't Let the World Pull You In

Meditate on the following scripture -

Proverbs 3:5-6 "Trust in the LORD with all your heart And do not lean on your own understanding. ⁶ In all your ways acknowledge Him, And He will make your paths straight" (NASB)

It's so easy Father to get intimidated by the people of this world when we take our eyes off you and give ear to what they have to say. They speak lies that sound like the truth and make us feel foolish because we do not manage our marriage and life as they do. Help us Father to trust you completely, especially when we are bombarded with the logic that the world has to offer. Help us Father to become rooted in Your Word, so that we will not become unstable when we hear the idle reports of those who do not know you.

Take the following into consideration –

God commands husbands to love their wives and wives to respect their husbands for the proper development of the marriage. He did not give us this commandment because it was a good idea but because it was necessary.

Joe Robinson

REFLECTIONS

Write about how this prayer and passage of scripture can help you and your spouse overcome the teasing and ridicule of those who try to persuade you to live outside of God's plan for your marriage.

REFLECTIONS

(10) Principle: Pray and Expect God to Help You Resolve Your Unresolved Conflicts

A Date with Your Sweetheart (Wife)

Can you think of the last time that you and your wife went out on a date without the Children or anyone else tagging along? If you are like most of us it's probably been awhile since you and your wife were able to make a date night official, especially with the million and one things that has to be done. Things like the children, church, careers, hobbies, and the various other details that can and do hinder you from spending well needed time (Date) with your sweetheart (Wife).

I realize that this may be a scary thought for you and your wife. Why do I say that, because my wife and I have gone through that cycle. I can recall more than one instance where we finally made the necessary arrangements to go out on a date only to return home angry and frustrated with each another. We started out innocently talking in the car about nothing too important when all of a sudden, a controversial subject would lead us to an argument, and before you knew it, one of us was saying, "If this is how it's going to be we might as well go home". Is this a familiar phrase?

You and your wife will have to learn to get pass this hurdle. God does not take pleasure in seeing you and your wife neglecting to spend quality time together, because you are afraid that the outcome of the time spent together will have negative results. Yes, no one wants to go through the pains that are the results of hateful and harmful statements made through unhealthy marital conflict. You and your wife will have to do something about this. Understand, this will not happen overnight and that it will take work on your behalf, along with your sweetheart (Wife).

Consider the following scriptures –

Proverbs 14:29 "He who is slow to anger has great understanding, but he who has a quick temper displays folly." (WEB)

Proverbs 19:11 – "A man's discretion makes him slow to anger, And it is his glory to overlook a transgression." (NASB)

Ephesians 4:32 – "And be kind to one another, tenderhearted, forgiving each other, just as God also in Christ forgave you" (WEB)

Colossians 3:12-13 "[12]So, as those who have been chosen of God, holy and beloved, put on a heart of compassion, kindness, humility, gentleness and patience; [13]bearing with one another, and forgiving each other, whoever has a complaint against anyone; just as the Lord forgave you, so also should you." (NASB)

Heavenly Father for those who will find this difficult to put into action, please help them to surrender their hearts to you concerning this matter.

Take the following into consideration –

Sometimes your spouse will not see your point of view concerning a matter that's important to you. This does not mean that they will not have a change of heart later as you pray for them and allow God to work to produce a change when it is necessary.

Joe Robinson

REFLECTIONS

Write about how you and your spouse can use the scriptures that you have just read to sort out the difficulties of spending time together.

The Color of Marriage

REFLECTIONS

(11) Principle: Be Willing to Change

You have developed patterns of behaviors that you have become accustom to. Now is the time for you to recognize all behaviors that are not beneficial to your marriage becoming what God commands it to be.

Consider the following scriptures -

Romans 13:14 "But put on the Lord Jesus Christ, and make no provision for the flesh, to gratify its desires." (ESV)

Psalm 51:5 "Behold, I was brought forth in iniquity. In sin my mother conceived me." (WEB)

Psalm 51:7 "Purge me with hyssop, and I shall be clean; wash me, and I shall be whiter than snow." (ESV)

Ephesians 5:8 "for you were formerly darkness, but now you are Light in the Lord; walk as children of Light" (ESV)

Romans 13:12 "The night is far spent, the day is at hand: let us therefore cast off the works of darkness, and let us put on the armor of light." (WEB)

Also read **Ephesians 2:2-3**

REFLECTIONS

We are back on behaviors once again. Write about the behaviors that you have changed or are changing for the betterment of your marriage.

Joe Robinson

REFLECTIONS

(11) Prayer for Be Willing to Change

Meditate on the following scripture -

Galatians 5:16 "But I say, walk by the Spirit, and you will not gratify the desires of the flesh." (ESV)

Heavenly Father, thank you for giving me the ability through your Holy Spirit to change all of my behaviors that are not beneficial to my marriage. Help me to recognize these behaviors and please give me the desire and willingness to change them as well. As I look at (your spouse's name) may I be reminded to change any behavior that creates a wedge between the two of us. I pray this in the name of Jesus, amen.

Take the following into consideration –

Your marriage will not get better until you get better at making it better.

Joe Robinson

REFLECTIONS

Write about how this prayer and passage of scripture can help you and your spouse continue to change behaviors that benefit your marriage.

The Color of Marriage

REFLECTIONS

(12) Principle: Do not let your prior experiences destroy the trust and intimacy of your marriage

Please do not use your past (and sometimes present) negative experiences to judge the behavior of your spouse. Just because a certain behavior of your spouse brings up negative feelings and emotions that are connected to a pass negative experience in your life, it does not make them guilty unless you have actual proof that they are. Remember your spouse should remain innocent unless proven guilty, just as it is in a court of law. Give your spouse the benefit of the doubt before you accuse them of something that you think they have not done.

Consider the following scriptures –

James 1:5 – "But if any of you lacks wisdom, let him ask of God, who gives to all generously and without reproach, and it will be given to him". (NASB)

John 7:24 – "Do not judge according to appearance, but judge with righteous judgment." (WEB)

Ecclesiastes 7:8-9 "⁸Better is the end of a thing than its beginning. The patient in spirit is better than the proud in spirit. Don't be hasty in your spirit to be angry, for anger rests in the bosom of fools." (WEB)

Ephesians 6:11-12 – "¹¹Put on the whole armor of God, that you may be able to stand against the wiles of the devil. ¹²For our wrestling is not against flesh and blood, but against the principalities, against the powers, against the world's rulers of the darkness of this age, and against the spiritual forces of wickedness in the heavenly places" (WEB)

Galatians 5:25 - "If we live by the Spirit, let's also walk by the Spirit." (WEB)

Joe Robinson

REFLECTIONS

Write about how your past experiences may be affecting the trust and intimacy of your marriage in a negative way.

The Color of Marriage

REFLECTIONS

(12) Prayer for Do not let your prior experiences destroy the trust and intimacy of your marriage

Meditate on the following scripture

1 Samuel 16:7 "But the LORD said to Samuel, "Do not look at his appearance or at the height of his stature, because I have rejected him; for God sees not as man sees, *for man looks at the outward appearance, but the LORD looks at the heart.*"" (NASB)

Father God, help me to know the truth that I ought to know instead of making quick judgments about (your spouse's name) behavior based on my feelings and past experiences. I ask that you teach me how to transform my mind and react differently when my feelings and emotions from past experiences try to dictate the outcome of (your spouse's name) behaviors. Thank you for healing our marriage of this unfair practice. LORD, even though my feelings and experiences may prove to be correct at times, I know that I must still depend on you instead of depending on my own point of view and being wise in my own eyes. It is in Jesus' name that I pray. Amen

Take the following into consideration –

Fairness is a valuable tool that can adjust your spouse's attitude toward you.

REFLECTIONS

Write about how this prayer and passage of scripture can help you and your spouse maintain the intimacy and trust of your marriage by not allowing past experiences to judge each other's behaviors.

Joe Robinson

REFLECTIONS

(13) Principle: Do not let your prior experiences destroy the trust and intimacy of your marriage: Part II

Please do not let your concealed past (and sometimes present) negative experiences hinder or destroy the trust and intimacy of your marriage. These are your negative experiences that are no longer at the forefront of your life and are locked away in your heart making them a functional part of who you are. The real-to-life feelings and emotions associated with these locked away negative experiences can be unlocked at any time by certain words, actions, or behaviors that are carried out by your spouse. Many times you will not be aware when they are being unlocked.

When these negative feelings and emotions are unlocked and transferred back to the forefront of your life, the memory associated with these experience(s) most likely will not be unlocked with them. Because of this, you will in all probability attribute your lack of passion, negative responses, ill feelings, and other negative reactions to something that your spouse has done when in fact this more than likely is not the logic at all.

At this point, unless you decide to think before you react, all of the negative feelings and emotions associated with the past experience(s) will be used against your spouse who will have no idea of what is happening; and most of the time neither will you.

Joe Robinson

Consider the following scriptures

Proverbs 4:23 "Watch over your heart with all diligence, For from it flow the springs of life" (NASB)

1 Peter 5:8 "Be sober and self-controlled. Be watchful. Your adversary, the devil, walks around like a roaring lion, seeking whom he may devour." (WEB)

Psalm 4:4 "Be angry, and do not sin; ponder in your own hearts on your beds, and be silent. Selah" (ESV)

1 Corinthians 13 "Finally, brothers, rejoice. Aim for restoration, comfort one another, agree with one another, live in peace; and the God of love and peace will be with you."(ESV)

REFLECTIONS

Considering what you have just read, write about how your concealed previous experiences could be affecting the quality of your marriage. Now that you are aware that your concealed previous experiences could be affecting the quality of your marriage, start recognizing and pointing them out when you begin to realize that certain events from your past could be affecting the trust and intimacy of your marriage.

Joe Robinson

REFLECTIONS

(13) Prayer for Do not let your prior experiences destroy the trust and intimacy of your marriage: Part II

Meditate on the following scripture –

Psalm 139:4 "Even before there is a word on my tongue, Behold, O LORD, You know it all."

God I may not completely understand all that is involved in the way that I think or behave at times. This is why I ask you now to help me to get a better understanding. When I feel ill towards (enter your spouse's name) may you help me to understand why I am behaving this way and help me to control what I do and or say to (enter your spouse's name). I have been through a lot in my past, much of which I do not remember, but you remember and I thank you for helping me to not let my past, corrupt my present and future with (enter your spouse's name). I pray this in Jesus name, amen.

Take the following into consideration –

Turning thoughts of the imagination into a real life ordeal that has never taken place will produce in you the feelings and emotions that are associated with that imaginary ordeal. So, the next time you find yourself acting out a conflict in your mind that includes your spouse doing something that may or may not happen, dismiss the thought right away before you find yourself reacting negatively towards your spouse who hasn't done anything wrong.

Joe Robinson

REFLECTIONS

Write about how this prayer and passage of scripture can help you and your spouse understand how unknown past experiences can be affecting the trust and intimacy of your marriage.

REFLECTIONS

(14) Principle: God will test you in the areas of your marriage where He requires you to change or grow

You will never know when or how much you have changed or grown unless you are tested in the area of your marriage where growth or change is required. So, the next time God uses the normal activities of your marriage to test your growth or change, strive to receive a passing grade.

Consider the following scriptures –

Proverbs 17:3 "The refining pot is for silver and the furnace for gold, But the LORD tests hearts." (NASB)

Psalm 17:3 "You have tried my heart; You have visited me by night; You have tested me and You find nothing; I have purposed that my mouth will not transgress" (NASB)

Jeremiah 17:10 ""I, the LORD, search the heart, I test the mind, Even to give to each man according to his ways, According to the results of his deeds." (NASB)

Psalm 26:2 "Examine me, O LORD, and try me; Test my mind and my heart" (NASB)

REFLECTIONS

Write about how God has tested your marriage; be sure to write about what you learned from the test as well as what you learned from the outcome of the test.

Joe Robinson

REFLECTIONS

(14) Prayer for God will test you in the areas of your marriage where He requires you to change or grow.

Meditate on the following scripture

Psalm 139:23-24 "²³ Search me, O God, and know my heart; Try me and know my anxious thoughts ²⁴ And see if there be any hurtful way in me, And lead me in the everlasting way." (NASB)

Heavenly Father I confess that I do not always pass the tests that you have given me. I also must confess that I sometimes purposely fail the test because of my selfishness. Help me in this area Father, teach me what I need to know and most of all give me the desire to pass the tests in the areas where I need to grow or change. It is in the name of Jesus your Son I pray, Amen.

Take the following into consideration –

It takes total commitment to see a marriage through. If you are not totally committed to your marriage there is a greater chance that anything could come along and destroy your marriage. Therefore, make sure that your marriage starts and ends with Jesus who is able to sustain your marriage until the end.

Joe Robinson

REFLECTIONS

Write about how this prayer and passage of scripture can help you and your spouse prepare for and pass the test that God will administer in your marriage.

REFLECTIONS

(15) Principle: God Can See Things That You Cannot (Walk In The Spirit)

Can you think of a time when you had an intense desire to have something, or to accomplish a particular project and it turned out to be something that you did not need to have or should not have done? I know I have. Some time ago I had an intense desire to purchase a new van for our family. The source of this desire came from my evaluation of the two vehicles that we already had and my belief that our finances would allow us to take on this extra expense.

I had convinced myself that neither of the vehicles that we had was suitable transportation for my wife and children. The air conditioning was not working properly and a creaking sound was coming from the front end of the 2003 Kia van that we had just financed no longer than 6 months before my desire. My wife was not thoroughly convinced that we should purchase a new van. She considered the Kia to be in good working condition and was content with the state of the a/c. The 1996 Isuzu that I was driving had been running well with the exception of the blower fan not operating. My concern with the Isuzu was not having heat while driving during the winter months when the temperature would drop.

At the time of the desire, I acted upon it instantly by securing financing for the vehicle through our credit union. I also calculated the payment of the vehicle into the budget and was sure that we had enough income in the bank to cover things if something went wrong. Now let me not forget to mention that I was going to be getting a pay raise in seven months and I factored that into the equation as well.

That next morning my wife and I got up and arranged for childcare, and we were on our way to fulfill the intense desire of mine to replace the minivan that we had with a brand new vehicle that would relieve me of all of my concerns. We set the alarm, left the house, and got into the Kia that I thought for sure would break down at anytime. As I started the van and drove off, I listened and waited for the confirmation that would assure me that we were in need of a new van. As we drove out of the driveway the silence and the smooth operation of the vehicle caused me to rethink my position on the reliability of the van. I am not sure if I said anything to my wife, but at the time I began to realize that my assumptions about the van were false. Quickly my reasoning for getting the van changed from a standpoint of reliability to; I want my wife to have a new van to drive.

Well to sum everything up, we were able to get a brand new 2011 van the next day. I drove the van home that night and as I went to bed, I was not able to sleep. I prayed and asked God to reverse the process if this was not what we needed, and soon after that I found peace and fell asleep. The next morning as I got ready for work the finance manager called and wanted me to come back into the dealership to tie up some loose ends. When I got there he informed me that the company that financed the vehicle wanted money down and that was my ticket out. God had answered my prayer and the prayer of my wife as well.

As time went on, I came to realize why God did not want me to get the new van. He knew what would happen in the future that I could not see. He knew that even though I would get a raise, He also knew that my hours would be cut from 40 hours a week to 32. He knew that we would struggle with the payment and I thank Him for changing the circumstances and speaking to me about not getting the van. I especially thank my wife for allowing me to go through this gracefully and for praying that God's will would be done.

I learned three things from this.

1. I should listen to the voice of the Holy Spirit as He makes an effort to counter the faulty desires of my old nature.
2. I should never manage my way through decisions that are based on my feelings and emotions that may seem to be authentic, but are not based on reliable facts.
3. I should listen and act accordingly when I see that my reasoning for making a decision has failed.

Consider the Following Scripture

Galatians 5:16 "This I say then, Walk in the Spirit, and you shall not fulfill the lust of the flesh."

Take the following into consideration -

Our old nature wars against our new nature all the time. When you have a longing or desire to do or have something, you should first pray, consult with your spouse, and listen to the voice of the Holy Spirit just in case He has to give you information to counter the lust and desires of your old nature.

REFLECTIONS

Write about how you can prevent making bad decisions by praying, listening to the Holy Spirit, and ignoring irrational desires.

Joe Robinson

REFLECTIONS

Closing remarks

I would like to applaud you and your spouse or future spouse for taking the time and putting forth the effort to complete this Christian marriage-learning guide. At this point you have replenished your marriage by infusing it with principles and concepts from the Word of God that will help you and your spouse maintain a healthy long-lasting biblical marriage that pleases God and brings Him glory. Now that you are done, I recommend that you continue the process of replenishing your marriage. Visit our site, www.thecolorofmarriage.com, to find out how you can continue the process of replenishing your marriage.

Made in the USA
Lexington, KY
15 August 2018